**W9-AEC-049**

# BICYCLES

## WHEELS IN MOTION

Morgan Hughes

Rourke

Publishing LLC

Vero Beach, Florida 32964

www.rourkepublishing.com

PHOTO CREDITS: Cover courtesy of RazorUSA; title page Mark Wilson/Getty Images; p 4 Kevin Moloney/Getty Images; p 8, 18, 21 Pat McBeth; p 15 Stanley Chou/Getty Images; p 17 Mike Simons/Getty Images

Title page: *Biking is a wonderful way for families to spend time together.*

Editor: Frank Sloan

Cover design by Nicola Stratford

### Library of Congress Cataloging-in-Publication Data

Hughes, Morgan, 1957-
 Bicycles / Morgan Hughes.
     v. cm. — (Wheels in motion)
Includes bibliographical references and index.
Contents: Bicycles in the beginning — BMX bikes — Mountain bikes — Road bikes — Stunt bikes — Extreme biking — Cross-country biking — Equipment and repairs — Safety tips.
 ISBN 1-58952-665-1 (hardcover)
 1. Cycling—Juvenile literature. 2. Bicycles—Juvenile literature.
[1. Bicycles and bicycling.] I. Title. II. Series: Hughes, Morgan, 1957-   Wheels in motion.
 GV1043.5.H84 2003
 796.6—dc21

                                                         2003004053

Printed in the USA

CG/CG

# Table of Contents

# Bicycles in the Beginning

Bicycling has been a favorite American **pastime** for more than 100 years. It was in the late 1800s that a man named John Kemp Starley built a bicycle with a chain-driven rear wheel. Starley's design also put the rider much closer to the ground, unlike bicycles with enormous front wheels and a tiny back wheel.

*Old fashioned "big wheel" bikes weren't just for big people.*

# BMX Bikes

The initials **BMX** stand for bicycle motocross. These are very sturdy "muscle" bikes, usually fitted with **suspension** systems to absorb tremendous shock. BMX bikes are designed for dirt tracks. They have a simple one-gear design. They usually feature 20-inch (50-centimeter) wheels, which are best for handling and turning stability.

*Kids of all ages race side by side on the BMX trail.*

# Mountain Bikes

Mountain bikes are for adventurous riders who want to avoid the traffic of the street and explore trails and rugged natural **terrain**. Mountain bikes usually have fat tires and come with at least 21 gears (for climbing up steep heels). They also feature suspension systems for both the front and rear wheels.

*Mountain bikes can take you anywhere, on road or off, rain or shine.*

# Road Bikes

Road bikes are built for speed and distance. They have skinny tires and lightweight **frames**. These bikes are designed so the rider is somewhat hunched over forward to cut down on wind resistance. Standard road bikes have between 16 and 20 gears, with gear shifters built into the brake handles for safety and convenience.

*Mothers and daughters can hit the road together.*

*Proper protective equipment will make for a happier biking experience.*

*Recumbent bikes allow the rider to sit much lower to the ground.*

# Stunt Bikes

Stunt bikes are small and lightweight and look a lot like BMX bikes. They have a specially designed head set (or steering tube), which allows the handlebars to spin 360 degrees. The rear axle features "pegs," which riders can stand on during their tricks. That is why these are sometimes called "peg bikes."

*"Wheel stands" are standard— but very difficult— "rad" bike stunts.*

# Extreme Biking

There is more and more popularity in **extreme** biking, which shares some of the features of extreme skateboarding and in-line skating. Bikers use ramps, half-pipes, and other man-made and natural obstacles to execute tricks. Extreme biking can be very dangerous and is suggested only for expert bicycle riders.

*Extreme bikers take a lot of chances, but deliver lots of thrills.*

# Cross-country Biking

Cross-country is a very exciting and challenging sport that combines mountain biking and a mixture of hiking and **steeplechase**. It requires racers to ride over a difficult mountain bike course. Then, when the terrain becomes too difficult, racers must carry their bicycles on their backs to the next stretch they can ride.

*When there's no road or path, carrying your bike is the only option.*

# Equipment and Repairs

With a little time and patience, anybody can become a capable bike **mechanic**. But to do so, you must have the right tools and equipment. A good bike shop will stock all the basic cleaning fluids and **maintenance** tools. The shop will also have answers to any questions you may have about how to keep your wheels in motion.

*Take the time to clean your bike and it will last longer and work better.*

FINISH
LINE™
Premium
**EcoTech²**
Cleaner
Degreaser

A Bio-Cl___
Break___ O__

► **Totally Solvent Free**
► **Outperforms Traditional Cleaners**
► **Non-irritating, No Fumes**
► **100% Biodegradable & Nont___**

full strength!

Flammable

20 oz.

WHITE
LIGHTNING
**CLEAN
STREAK**
METAL-PREP

► Quickly dissolves oil
grease, grime and m___

► Dries rapidly lea___
no residue!

► Prepares surface___
lubricant and en___
metal adhesion!

Flammable. Keep Out of Re___
12.5 fl.oz. / 350 ml
Read precautions on ___

PEDRO'S
**BIKE
LUST**
SILICONE POLISH

Superior shine and protection from water & UV ra___
Residual film makes future cleaning easier.
Made from the finest ingredients.

Lustrant supérieur protégeant de l'eau et des UV ___
Laisse un film protecteur facilitant le nettoyage.
Fabriqué à partir d'éléments de haute qualité.

Superior brillo y protección contra el agua y los ra___
ultravioleta.
Su capa residual facilita la limpieza en el futuro.
Fabricado con los más finos ingredientes.

DANGER; CAUTION - EYE IRRITANT
Read carefully other cautions of the rear panel.
___ oz/250 ml   Made in USA.

SHAKE WELL • SHAKE WELL • SHAKE

**RITCHEY**
BICYCLE COMPONENTS

**CHAIN LUBE**

Cleans and Lubes
in one step

Shake Well Before Using

**PRO**

4oz. Danger: Flammable, read warning
Keep out of reach of Children

ORIGINAL
**WHITE
LIGHTNING**®

**Self-Cleaning™
Wax Lubricant**

► Patented dirt "shedding" formula

► Chain, derailleurs & gears stay
clean, work better, last longer.

**#1 SELLING LUBE IN USA!**

4 FL oz / 120 ml  • Flammable, Read cautions on back.

**PEDRO'S**

**SYN
LUBE
ROAD**

Synthetic Road
Chain Lube

DANGER: HARMFUL IF SWALLOWED ___

Please
Recycle

___
59 ml

# Safety Tips

No matter what kind of bike you ride, the most important piece of equipment is your helmet. It should fit you snugly and carry a certification sticker from the Consumer Product Safety Commission (CPSC). Because of the materials used in the inner protective shell, the helmet should be replaced at least every three to five years.

# Glossary

**BMX** (BEE EM ECKS) — stands for "bicycle motocross"

**extreme** (ecks TREEM) — beyond the normal, expected level; very intense

**frames** (FRAYMZ) — the systems of tubing that act as the bicycle's skeleton

**mechanic** (muh KAN ick) — one who can build, assemble, or repair a machine, like a bike

**maintenance** (MAIN tuh nents) — the work of keeping something in working order

**pastime** (PASS time) — an activity that uses one's spare time pleasantly

**steeplechase** (STEE puhl CHAYS) — a race over varied terrain and different obstacles

**suspension** (suss PEN shun) — a system using heavy duty springs as shock absorbers

**terrain** (TUR RAIN) — the character of an area of land (hilly, rocky, etc.)

# Index

## Further Reading

Bibbins, Neil. *Bikes, Scooters, Skates, and Boards.* Storey Books
    Publishing, 2002
Eckert, Edana. *I Can Ride a Bike.* Children's Press, 2002
Kalman, Bobbie, et al. *Cycling In Action.* Crabtree Publishing, 2002
Roberts, Oliver. *How to Get Wheely Fit.* Barrons Educational Series, 2003

## Websites To Visit

www.bikexprt.com/streetsmarts/
dir.yahoo.com/Recreation/Sports/Cycling
www.bicyclinglife.com

## About The Author

Morgan Hughes is the author of more than 50 books on hockey, track and
field, bicycling, and many other subjects. He is also an avid cyclist and professional
musician currently living with his family in Connecticut.